SHAPING MODERN SCIENCE

What Is Cell Theory?

Marina Cohen

Crabtree Publishing Company

www.crabtreebooks.com

SHAPING MODERN SCIENCE

Author: Marina Cohen
Publishing plan research and development:
 Sean Charlebois, Reagan Miller
 Crabtree Publishing Company
Editors: Sara Cohen Christopherson,
 Adrianna Morganelli
Proofreaders: Kristine Lindsay, Molly Aloian
Project coordinator: Kathy Middleton
Editorial services: Clarity Content Services
Production coordinator and prepress technician:
 Katherine Berti
Print coordinator: Katherine Berti
Series consultant: Eric Walters
Cover design: Katherine Berti
Design: First Image
Photo research: Linda Tanaka
Photographs: cover/title page Shutterstock; p4 Aksenova Natalya/Shutterstock; p5 Jubal Harshaw/Shutterstock; p6 top from page 377 of "The Story of Nineteenth-Century Science" by Henry Smith Williams/public domain/wiki, Portrait of Schleiden/Fotografie von Carl Schenk/public domain/wiki; p7 National Institutes of Health/US Dept. of Health and Human Services; p8 myrthe krook/iStock; p9 left CoolKoon licensed under the Creative Commons Attribution 3.0 Unported license, User Fir0002 on en.wikipedia/GNU Free Documentation License; p10 Dave White/iStock; p12 Public domain/wiki; p13 Sebastian Kaulitzki/iStock; p14 Billings Microscope Collection/National Museum of Health and Medicine/AFIP; p15 Public domain/wiki; p16 Naturalis/National Museum of Natural History/public domain/wiki; p17 left Public domain/wiki, Jeroen Rouwkema licensed under the Creative Commons Attribution-Share Alike 3.0 Unported license; p19 top Mariana Ruiz Villarreal/LadyofHats/wiki, Messer-Woland and Szczepan1990 licensed under the Creative Commons Attribution-Share Alike 3.0 Unported license; p20 archives/iStock; p21 Hans Hillewaert licensed under the Creative Commons Attribution-Share Alike 3.0 Unported license; lower Lightspring/Shutterstock; p22 top Fenne kustermans/iStock, Karl Dolenc/iStock; p23 Mariana Ruiz Villarreal/LadyofHats/wiki; p24 Lisa Thornberg/iStock; p25 top Kristian Peters/Fabelfroh/GFDL-wiki, SuperManu/GFDK-wiki; p26 Original image appeared in "T Cells Cause Lung Damage in Emphysema" PLoS Med 1(1): e25/Licensed under the Creative Commons Attribution 2.0 Generic license; p27 left Karl Dolenc/iStock, Jon Sullivan/public domain/wiki; p28 irink/Shutterstock; p29 Public domain/wiki; pps 30-31 Bruce Iverson; p33 R.K. Webster/USDA; p34 Public domain/wiki; p35 Sebastian Kaulitzki/Shutterstock; p36 top creativei images/Shutterstock, Dmitry Knorre/iStock; p37 Monika Wisniewska/Shutterstock; p38 martan/Shutterstock; p39 Dr.Mae Melvin/CDC; p40 Michael Taylor/Shutterstock; p41 inset wiki; p41 Jubal Harshaw/Shutterstock; p42 Quasar Jarosz at en.wikipedia/Creative Commons Attribution-Share Alike 3.0 Unported license; p43 sgame/iStock; p44 Patrick J. Lynch, medical illustrator; C. Carl Jaffe, MD, cardiologist/Creative Commons Attribution 2.5 License; p45 top Dr. Tsuji Yuuji/Creative Commons Attribution-Share Alike 2.5 Generic license, Michael Abbey/Photo Researchers, Inc.; p47 LadyofHats/public domain/wiki; p48 Dreamy Girl/Shutterstock; p50 Darryl Leja/Courtesy of National Human Genome Research Institute; p51 Martin McCarthy/iStock; p52 Roy van Heesbeen/public domain/wiki; p53 Russ London at en.wikipedia licensed under the Creative Commons Attribution-Share Alike 3.0 Unported license; p54 left Courtesy of Rockefeller University, Joan Wright Goodman; p55 left Courtesy of Presidenza della Repubblica, Rama/Creative Commons Attribution-Share Alike 2.0 France license; p56 Public domain/USDA; p57 BioMedical/Shutterstock

---

Library and Archives Canada Cataloguing in Publication

Cohen, Marina
 What is cell theory? / Marina Cohen.

(Shaping modern science)
Includes index.
Issued also in electronic format.
ISBN 978-0-7787-7199-9 (bound).--ISBN 978-0-7787-7206-4 (pbk.)

 1. Cells--Juvenile literature. 2. Cytology--Juvenile literature.
I. Title. II. Series: Shaping modern science

QH582.5.C65 2011   j571.6   C2011-900182-9

Library of Congress Cataloging-in-Publication Data

Cohen, Marina, 1967-
 What is cell theory? / Marina Cohen.
  p. cm. -- (Shaping modern science)
 Includes index.
 ISBN 978-0-7787-7206-4 (pbk. : alk. paper) --
 ISBN 978-0-7787-7199-9 (reinforced library binding :
 alk. paper) -- ISBN 978-1-4271-9528-9 (electronic (pdf))
 1. Cells--Juvenile literature. 2. Cytology--Juvenile literature.
 I. Title. II. Series.

 QH582.5.C65 2011
 571.6--dc22
                                        2010052633

Crabtree Publishing Company

www.crabtreebooks.com   1-800-387-7650

Printed in the U.S.A./022011/CJ20101228

Published in Canada
Crabtree Publishing
616 Welland Ave.
St. Catharines, ON
L2M 5V6

Published in the United States
Crabtree Publishing
PMB 59051
350 Fifth Avenue, 59th Floor
New York, New York 10118

Published in the United Kingdom
Crabtree Publishing
Maritime House
Basin Road North, Hove
BN41 1WR

Published in Australia
Crabtree Publishing
386 Mt. Alexander Rd.
Ascot Vale (Melbourne)
VIC 3032

Contents

There are no
biological cells in
cell phones.

What Is Cell Theory?

You can build a house out of wood or bricks. You can bake a cake if you have flour, sugar, butter, milk, and eggs. But how do you build a human being? What are plants and animals made of? These are questions ancient philosophers debated thousands of years ago.

Today, we know that all living things on Earth are made up of very tiny parts. These parts are called cells. Cells are the building blocks of life. Every living thing—from turtles to trees, cherries to chickens—is made up of cells. All new cells come from cells that already exist. This, essentially, is what the Cell **Theory** is all about.

Now it all seems simple enough, right? But remember, we didn't always have the technology we have today. New technologies helped people make new observations. Over hundreds of years, and with the contributions of many scientists and researchers, the Cell Theory took shape. Today, scientists continue to learn new things about cells.

↑ Your cells are very similar to the cells of this chicken.

Scientific Theory or Law?

In science, a *theory* is a well-tested set of ideas that explains how something occurs. For example, many kinds of evidence together support the Cell Theory. A scientific *law* describes how something consistently happens under certain conditions. For example, the law of gravity describes how objects fall to Earth's surface.

Quick fact

Your body is made up of about 50 trillion cells.

So when and how were cells discovered? What do they look like? Where do they come from? It would take some pretty radical ideas, some cool inventions, exciting discoveries, and overcoming a lot of resistance before scientists would have the answers we accept today.

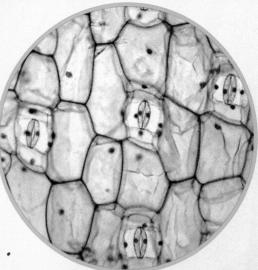

↑ This photo shows the cells on the surface of a leaf.

"If we examine the accomplishments of man in his most advanced endeavors . . . we find that the cell has done all this long before him, with greater resourcefulness and much greater efficiency."

—Albert Claude, Nobel Lecture, "The Coming Age of the Cell," December 12, 1974

Quick fact

There are no biological cells in cell phones.

What Is a Scientific Theory?

Scientists begin by making observations and learning what is already known about a topic. Using this background information and their observations, a scientist develops a question about the topic. Then, a scientist comes up with a possible answer to that question, or a **hypothesis**. Next, a scientist may conduct tests, run experiments, and make additional observations to collect evidence. The evidence may support the hypothesis or it may refute the hypothesis. If evidence from many experiments and studies over many years all support the hypothesis, then the hypothesis eventually becomes a theory. A theory can be modified if new evidence requires it. It can also be discarded if evidence turns up to refute it.

Three Amazing Scientists

Schwann

Theodor Schwann was born in 1810 in Neuss—what was then Rhenish Prussia, but is now Germany. He was the son of a goldsmith and printer, and inherited his father's love of mechanics. As a boy, he constructed a variety of little machines. He studied first in Cologne, then later in Bonn where he met Johannes Müller. Schwann helped Müller with his **physiological** experiments. Schwann was one of the first to challenge the principle of vitalism and work toward a physical explanation of life.

Schleiden

Born in 1804, Matthias Jakob Schleiden was a **botanist**. He was one of the first German biologists to break with traditional beliefs and accept Charles Darwin's **Theory of Evolution**. In his writings, Schleiden confirmed what was, at the time, just an informal hypothesis—that the various parts of a plant were all composed of cells. Schwann, extending Schleiden's ideas to animal cells, developed the beginnings of the Cell Theory.

Virchow

Rudolph Karl Virchow was born in Prussia in the province of Pomerania, which is now part of Poland. He became a doctor and, like Schwann, worked under Johannes Müller. Virchow's research would disprove one of Schwann's hypotheses, and so contribute to the Cell Theory as we know it today.

Vitalism

Vitalism has its roots in ancient Egypt. It is the belief that there is a mysterious inner force or energy that gives living things life. Vitalists believe that there is something beyond the physical and chemical explanations to life. It is known as *Chi* in China, *Prana* in India, and various names in other cultures. Vitalism was the dominant belief prior to the discovery of the cell and the development of the Cell Theory.

CHAPTER ONE

The Marvelous Microscope!

A Whole New World

In ancient Greece, long before Schwann, Schleiden, and Virchow, philosophers Democritus and Leucippus had a wild idea that would change the way people looked at the world. The two philosophers **postulated** that all solid matter—both living and non-living—was made up of very tiny particles that were invisible to the naked eye. Certainly, in a time where there was no technology to confirm such an idea, they would have met much resistance and perhaps even ridicule.

It would take another 2,000 years before an amazing little instrument called the microscope would be invented. The microscope is a tool used to see very tiny objects—objects far too small to see with the naked eye. Once in use, the microscope revealed a whole new world never seen before: the incredible tiny world of the cell.

But where did the idea of the microscope originate? Who invented it? How did it change and shape the world of science?

↑Curved glass bends light rays, changing the way an object's image appears.

A Chunk of Crystal

The idea of magnification must have begun at some distant point in history, most likely long before words and pictures were recorded. Imagine some clever person walking along a road or mountainside and noticing a chunk of transparent crystal lying on the ground. This person may have picked up the piece of crystal. It would have been thicker in the middle and thinner on its edges. When this person looked through the piece of crystal, objects would have appeared larger. And so the magnifying glass would eventually be born.

↑ *Notice that the light rays coming into the left side of the lens are parallel. As the light rays pass through this convex lens, they bend and converge, or come together, on the other side of the lens.*

Flea Glasses

The very first microscopes were nothing more than tubes with a piece of glass at the end. They could only magnify objects up to ten times their actual size. These tubes were mostly used to examine bugs and other such creatures and so they were given the nickname *flea glasses*.

↑ *Through this convex lens, objects appear smaller and upside down.*

Quick fact

The lens is named after the lentil seed because of its shape.

Hand Me My Glasses!

The invention of spectacles was a huge influence in the field of science. We don't know exactly who invented them, but Marco Polo saw elderly people using them during his visit to China in 1270. The Chinese, however, claim to have seen spectacles in use in Arabia even earlier than this. Although there is dispute as to their origin, it is agreed that at some time between 1268 and 1289, spectacles came to the western world. At first, they were owned mostly by monks. The monks held them in front of their eyes or balanced them on their noses while they transcribed books word by word. When books became more widely available, middle- and lower-class people began wearing spectacles as well. Spectacle-making became a thriving business. Spectacle-makers popped up throughout Europe and peddlers traveled town to town selling them.

↓Compound microscopes, like this one, have two lenses. One lens is in the eyepiece. The other lens is right above the object being examined.

Zacharias and Hans Janssen

In the 1590s, Dutch spectacle-maker Zacharias Janssen and his father Hans were experimenting with different lenses to create a more powerful magnification device. One design included two tubes that could slide out of an outer tube. Lenses were attached to each end of the moving tubes. To focus this early microscope, you had to slide the moving tube in or out. Another design had a large tube fixed to a base. Again, the tube had lenses on either end. Zacharias and Hans discovered that by using two lenses, nearby objects appeared much larger. Their experiments would eventually lead to the development of the compound microscope.

Two Lenses Are Better Than One!

The **compound microscope** uses two lenses and a source of light. The light illuminates the object being observed. When light passes through the object, the lens closest to it enlarges its image. The second lens—the one that you look into—acts as a magnifying glass and produces an even larger image than the one produced by the first lens. So, let's say the eyepiece lens can magnify objects by ten times and the lens closest to the object can magnify objects by forty times. 10 X 40 = 400. This means you can see the object 400 times larger.

Historical Footnote

The printing press was invented in the early to mid-1400s. This made books cheaper than copying them out by hand. Many people, not just the wealthy, could suddenly afford books and learned to read.

Quick fact

Early eye glass frames were made of leather, wood, horn, and even bone!

Early Microscopists

William Harvey was an English physician. In 1628, he described how blood circulates around the body. He also demonstrated the role our hearts play in pumping the blood. Many thought it was a crazy notion. It would take a microscope and a man by the name of Marcello Malpighi to help support Harvey's ideas.

Marcello Malpighi was an Italian physiologist. He is considered one of the first great **microscopists**. His discoveries would disprove a lot of ancient medical beliefs. Many people would bitterly and violently oppose him.

Malpighi was born in 1628. He got a degree in medicine and philosophy from the University of Bologna in 1653. He then became a professor in Pisa where he began his microscopic observations. Malpighi turned a critical eye on the physiological and medical theories of his day.

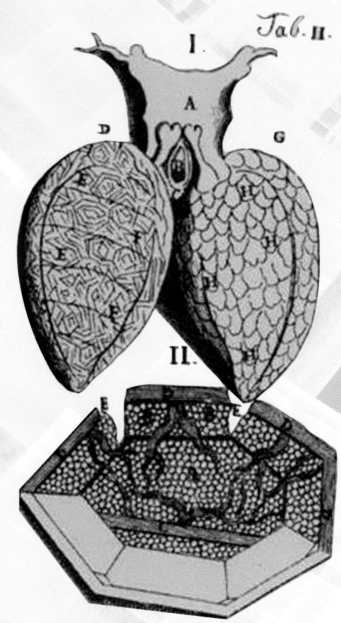

↑Marcello Malpighi drew this in the mid-1600s, after using a microscope to examine capillaries, or tiny blood vessels, in the lungs.

In 1661, he made his most important discovery. He described the system of **pulmonary capillaries** that carry blood from the **arteries** to the **veins**. Malpighi's careful microscopic observations confirmed William Harvey's ideas about blood circulation.

Although Malpighi didn't exactly get the microscopic functions of **organs** right, he did set the stage for cell theory. It was his discoveries of the hidden workings of **organisms** that forced physicians of the time to rethink their assumptions.

"All we know is still infinitely less than all that still remains unknown."

— William Harvey, 1628

→ *The work of William Harvey and Marcello Malpighi contributed to an understanding of how blood moves in the human body.*

Quick fact

The telescope was invented before the microscope. Galileo Galilei, an Italian **physicist**, mathematician, astronomer, and philosopher, called his instrument *occhiolino*, which means "little eye" in Italian.

Robert Hooke

King Charles II of England was interested in the microscope. He asked Sir Christopher Wren, a well-known architect and scientist, to do a series of microscopic studies. After a few presentations, Wren decided he was far too busy to continue. Along came a 26-year-old English scientist and inventor named Robert Hooke. Hooke accepted the assignment from Wren and began his microscopic observations.

Hooke was extremely gifted, especially with mechanics. He could recreate the entire mechanics of a clock out of wood, put them together and even make them work. He could also draw really well and could apply this skill to sketching his observations.

Hooke's technical knowledge allowed him to manipulate the height, angle, and light sources of his microscope. His tinkering allowed him to magnify objects by 50 times. This was an incredible feat when other microscopes of this time could only magnify objects by about ten times.

→ *Robert Hooke used a microscope that looked like this.*

A Thin Slice of Life

In 1665, Robert Hooke was studying a thin slice of cork. He noticed a lot of tiny compartments surrounded by walls. He named these tiny compartments *cellulae*, which means "little rooms" in Latin. The name *cells* stuck, and as a result, Hooke has been credited with discovering the first plant cells.

Hooke recorded his detailed drawings and observations in a book that sold far and wide. Though many scientists of the time recognized the importance of cells as the building blocks of life, it really wasn't until much later, in 1839, after Schwann and Schleiden, that the Cell Theory was generally accepted.

Robert Hooke and Isaac Newton argued over scientific matters. But in 1665, in a letter to Hooke, Newton expressed some appreciation for Hooke's work. He wrote:

"If I have seen further, it is by standing on the shoulders of giants."

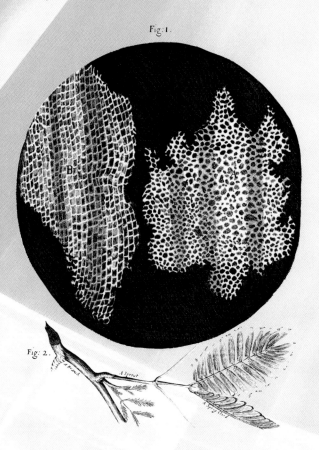

↑ *This sketch shows what Hooke saw when he examined a thin slice of cork under his microscope. Hooke thought these compartments looked like little rooms, so he called them cellulae.*

Quick fact

In 1666, a huge fire burned much of the city of London to the ground. Hooke was named London's surveyor and was given the task of rebuilding the city.

Antonie van Leeuwenhoek

Shortly after Hooke's discovery, a Dutch tradesman by the name of Antonie van Leeuwenhoek learned to grind lenses. He was able to greatly improve the techniques of the day. His lenses were a more pure glass, unlike the poor quality greenish ones of his contemporaries. Leeuwenhoek's lenses allowed him to invent a microscope that could magnify objects up to 270 times.

Animalcules

Although he had virtually no scientific education, Leeuwenhoek was inspired by Hooke's discovery of cells. With an open mind, free from the scientific **bias** of the day, Leeuwenhoek began observing pond water and other substances through one of his new improved microscopes. He noticed tiny things swimming around in the water. He called these *animalcules*. Hooke's observation of cork cells simply showed empty compartments. Hooke's cells were not moving. Leeuwenhoek's "little animals" were actually unicellular creatures—**bacteria** and **protozoa**.

↑ *Leeuwenhoek was the first person to see single-celled organisms.*

He reported his discovery to the Royal Society in 1678. Robert Hooke was asked by the Society to confirm Leeuwenhoek's findings. Once confirmed, this led to the idea that cells were actually alive. Leeuwenhoek had discovered animal cells. Both Hooke's and Leeuwenhoek's discoveries paved the way for Schwann, Schleiden, and Virchow and the Cell Theory.

"To Antonie van Leeuwenhoek...belongs the high merit of having been the first to use the microscope systematically and of having brought the construction of the simple microscope in his own hands to a high degree of perfection..."

—Arturo Castiglioni, medical historian

↓Below are drawings of Leeuwenhoek's microscope.
→The photo on the right shows a recreation of his microscope.

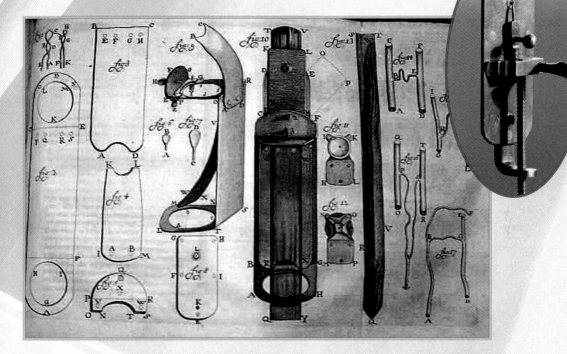

"Self-taught and never having attended a university, ignorant of Latin and Greek and of the classical texts, he became one of the greatest and most expert microscopists, thanks to the sagacity of his observations and the perfection of his technique."

—Arturo Castiglioni

CHAPTER TWO

What Are Cells?

The cell is the basic unit of life. Cells take in nutrients and get rid of waste. They grow and reproduce. Some cells can move, join with other cells, and communicate. The cell may be tiny, but it's pretty amazing. Some single cells can survive all by themselves. These are called **unicellular** organisms. Other organisms, like plants, animals, and humans, are **multicellular**. This means they are made up of many cells—in some cases, billions and even trillions of cells. All cells, however, can be divided into two basic groups: prokaryotes and eukaryotes.

Prokaryotes vs. Eukaryotes

Prokaryotic cells are cells that don't have a **nucleus**. They do have a large space called a **nucleoid**, in which their **genetic material** is contained. Prokaryotes have a large circular **chromosome** and a few smaller circular pieces called **plasmids**. The two kinds of prokaryotic cells are bacteria and **archaea**.

Eukaryotic cells are more organized cells. Instead of a nucleoid, eukaryotic cells keep all their chromosomes in a neat little compartment surrounded by its own **membrane**. This is called a nucleus. Eukaryotic cells make up plants and animals, including humans. They are about ten times as large as prokaryotic cells and can be almost 1,000 times greater in volume.

Both prokaryotic cells and eukaryotic cells have certain parts in common. They both have **plasma membranes**, **cytoplasm**, **cytoskeletons**, **ribosomes**, and chromosomes.

Quick fact

One hundred medium-sized prokaryotic cells lined up would be as thick as a sheet of paper!

→ *A prokaryotic cell (right) does not have a membrane-bound nucleus or other membrane-bound organelles. Stretched out, a prokaryote's genetic material, or DNA, would be in the shape of a circle.*

↓ *A eukaryotic cell (below) has a membrane-bound nucleus, as well as many other organelles. Your body is made up of cells like these.*

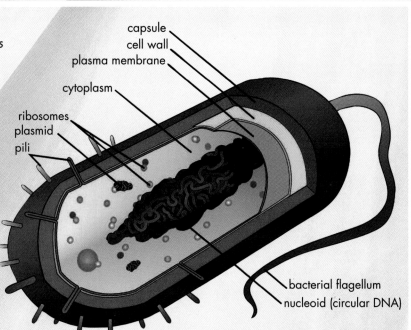

capsule
cell wall
plasma membrane
cytoplasm
ribosomes
plasmid
pili
bacterial flagellum
nucleoid (circular DNA)

mitochondria

nucleus

ribosome

rough endoplasmic reticulum (ER)

Golgi apparatus

smooth ER

Organelles

Only eukaryotic cells have a nucleus, mitochondria, and other membrane-bound **organelles**. The word *organelle* means "little organs" because they are to the cell as organs are to our bodies.

Did You Know?

Prokaryotic cells are tough! Some can survive in the freezing temperatures inside polar ice. Others can also live near volcanic vents reaching temperatures around 212°F (100°C).

Shape and Size

Cells come in all shapes and sizes. They can be shaped like rods, spheres, or spirals. Rods can be straight or curved. Spheres can be more oval than round. Spirals can be thick, thin, or even shaped like a comma. Some cells look like a splat of paint and others can change their shapes as they move. Plant cells usually look like boxes, while skin cells are flat. Nerve cells look like they have tentacles, while muscle cells are very thin. The size of a cell can also vary greatly. Ten thousand mycoplasmas (a type of bacteria) stacked on top of one another would only be as wide as a single strand of hair. Some cells are large and can be seen without a microscope. The yolk inside a bird's egg, for example, is actually a single cell.

Different kinds of cells are responsible for different jobs. Inside the human body, we have many types of cells. We have blood cells, bone cells, skin cells, and nerve cells, just to name a few. A cell's shape and size is linked to its job. For example, thin muscle cells contract and move bones.

Quick fact

The yolks of ostrich eggs are the largest single cells. They are the size of a baseball.

↓ *The nerve cells in a giraffe's neck are the longest cells—they can measure more than 9 feet 10 inches (3 meters).*

Did You Know?

The human brain is made up of about 100 million nerve cells. If you were to count them at the rate of one cell per second, it would take you 3,171 years!

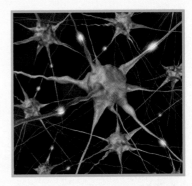

Animal Cells

Animal cells, including human cells, are eukaryotic cells. Animal cells have many parts in common with plant cells. Both animal and plant cells have a nucleus, cell membranes, cytoplasm, mitochondria, and **endoplasmic reticulum** (ER for short). Let's take a closer look at some of these parts and what they do.

Cell Membrane

The exterior layer of the cell is called the cell membrane, or plasma membrane. It is **semi-permeable**. This means certain things can enter and exit through it. Water, oxygen, and carbon dioxide can pass through the plasma membrane freely. The passage of larger **molecules**, such as sugar, is regulated.

Cytoplasm

This is the jelly-like substance inside the cell. It's about 65 percent water. The cytoplasm contains the organelles. Animal cells have more cytoplasm than plant cells.

↑Like all animals, this dog is made up of eukaryotic cells.

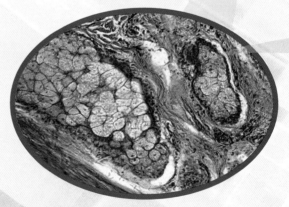

↑If you looked at the dog's skin under a microscope, you would see cells like these.

Mitochondria

Mitochondria are sausage-shaped structures in the cytoplasm of eukaryotic cells. They are responsible for changing food into energy, so they are often called the "power plant" of the cell.

Four Types of Tissue

The many types of animal cells can be categorized as one of just four types of tissue: **epithelial**, connective, muscle, or nerve.

Endoplasmic Reticulum

The endoplasmic reticulum (ER) is a series of membranes that zigzag through eukaryotic cells. The ER can be either rough or smooth. Rough ER has ribosomes embedded, giving it a dotted, or "rough," appearance. Proteins are made on the ribosomes embedded in the rough ER. These proteins move through the **Golgi apparatus** and are packaged to eventually get sent out of the cell. Proteins that remain in the cell are made on ribosomes that float free in the cytoplasm. The smooth ER makes **lipids**.

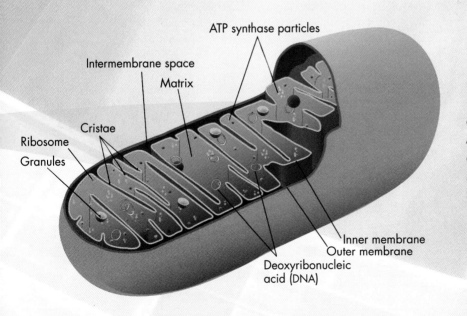

ATP synthase particles
Intermembrane space
Matrix
Cristae
Ribosome
Granules
Deoxyribonucleic acid (DNA)
Inner membrane
Outer membrane

←This organelle is a mitochondrion. Mitochondria break down sugars and release energy that the cell can use.

Plant Cells

Plants are a main food source for humans and other animals. They also produce oxygen through the process of **photosynthesis**. Robert Hooke is credited with the discovery of plant cells. Like animal cells, plant cells are eukaryotic. But plant cells have a few features that are not found in animal cells, including a **cell wall**, a large central **vacuole**, and **chloroplasts**.

Cell Wall

Plant cells have a tough layer outside their cell membranes called a cell wall. The cell wall provides the plant cell with its structure. This strong wall can be divided into two parts: the primary wall and the secondary wall. The secondary wall only forms once the cell has stopped growing.

↑ *Plants, like animals, are made up of eukaryotic cells, but plant cells differ from animal cells in several ways.*

"Any living cell carries with it the experience of a billion years of experimentation by its ancestors."

—Max Delbrück

Vacuole

The word vacuole actually means "empty space," but a plant cell's vacuole is not empty. Plant cells have a large central vacuole that takes up about 50-95 percent of the space inside the cell. By pressing outward against the cell wall, the vacuole helps keep a plant cell stable. This allows the plant to grow tall. The vacuole also serves as a space to store water, nutrients, and even waste. The vacuole can change its shape and size to suit the needs of the cell.

Chloroplasts

Chloroplasts are found in plant cells and in the cells of some other eukaryotes that conduct photosynthesis. Chloroplasts produce food for the cell. They take energy from the sun and convert it into sugars and starches through the process of photosynthesis. Like animal cells, plant cells also contain mitochondria. The mitochondria take the sugar produced by the chloroplasts and break it down to release energy that the cell can use.

↓ Chloroplasts capture the Sun's energy and convert it into energy that is stored in sugars and starches.

↑ These small green dots are chloroplasts, an organelle found in plant cells but not animal cells.

thylakoid

ribosome

chloroplast DNA

What's That Dark Spot?

Robert Brown (1773-1858) was a Scottish botanist. He made many important contributions to the study of plants and plant cells. He is credited with recognizing and naming the nucleus as a constant component of plant cells.

CHAPTER THREE

Developing the Cell Theory

When Hooke first described the cell, he had no idea these were the basic units of all living things. Although Antonie van Leeuwenhoek first observed and recorded unicellular creatures in the late 1600s, more than a hundred years would pass before people would make a connection between these single-celled organisms and cells in what we now know are multicellular organisms, such as animals.

Discovery of the Nucleus

The nucleus is the round spot found only in eukaryotic cells. It's like the cell's brain. Its discovery was an important step toward the development of the Cell Theory. The first description of the nucleus was made by Franz Bauer, an Austrian microscopist and artist, in 1802. However, it was botanist Robert Brown who, in 1831, would give the nucleus its name. Brown was examining orchids through a microscope when he noticed a dark spot. He named it the nucleus, but he didn't know its function.

↑ The dark spot in each cell is its nucleus. These cells have been stained to make the nuclei more easily visible.

Origin of New Cells

In 1832, Barthélemy Dumortier of France described cell division in plants. He observed a line forming between an original cell and a new cell being produced. Despite Dumortier's work, the origin of new cells remained controversial.

Schleiden and Schwann

In 1838, Matthias Jakob Schleiden formally stated that new plant cells formed in the nuclei of existing plant cells, though he did not know exactly how. One day, while Schleiden was dining with his friend, Theodor Schwann, the two got to chatting. Schwann was struck by the similarity of the structure of plant cells to those he had observed in animal tissue. The two raced back to Schwann's lab to look at his slides. They came to the conclusion that cells in plants and animals had much in common.

Schwann, therefore, extended Schleiden's ideas to animal cells and in 1839, he wrote a famous paper in which he declared that all living things are made up of cells. This led to the development of what he called the Cell Theory. Schwann's theory was based on three principles. He said that all living things are made up of cells; the cell is the smallest unit of life; and cells form spontaneously, much like crystals. Schwann didn't know it at the time, but his third principal was incorrect. It would, however, be an accepted idea for many years.

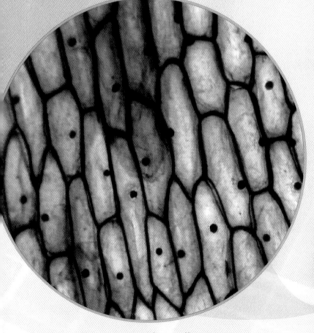

↑These onion skin cells were stained to show the nucleus, visible in each cell.

Quick fact

Theodor Schwann didn't acknowledge Matthias Schleiden or any other scientists who contributed to his ideas when he published his influential paper.

Virchow's Role

In 1858, Rudolf Virchow made another famous statement. His idea extended the work of Schwann and Schleiden. Virchow proposed that all living cells must come from cells that already exist. This was a radical notion at the time because most people, even scientists, still believed that non-living matter could turn into living tissue. This was called **spontaneous generation**.

Various experiments were thought to support the idea of spontaneous generation. For example, a piece of meat was observed. After some time, maggots would appear. People thought the maggots appeared out of nowhere. They did not realize that the maggots came from flies laying their eggs in the meat. Also, when John Turberville Needham heated various soupy concoctions, they all eventually grew life, such as mold. Again, his experiments supported the idea of spontaneous generation. Virchow, however, saw flaws in these experiments. With the help of the scientist Louis Pasteur, Virchow would firmly disprove the idea of spontaneous generation and so rewrite the third principle in Schwann's Cell Theory.

Using heat, Pasteur sterilized both the materials and the containers for his experiments. By doing so, he demonstrated that no new organisms would grow unless they were introduced into experiments. Pasteur established beyond any doubt the third principle of the Cell Theory.

Quick fact

In 1852, Robert Remak published his observations on cell division, providing evidence that Schleiden and Schwann were wrong about the origin of new cells. Virchow would later publicize his views without crediting Remak.

The Cell Theory

The discoveries of Schwann, Schleiden, and Virchow all contributed to the three basic principles of the Cell Theory, which still hold true today:

- All living things are made up of one or more cells.

- The cell is the smallest unit of life.

- All cells come from other cells that grow and divide.

↑Flies lay their tiny eggs on a dead animal. The eggs are so small, they may not be seen without magnification. The larvae come out of the eggs and start to eat the dead animal. As they grow, the larvae, or maggots, become easily noticeable.

A First Look at Chromosomes

Discovery of Mitosis

New staining techniques developed by Walther Flemming, a German cytologist, made it possible to view the process of cell division in great detail. Flemming named this process **mitosis**, which came from the Greek word for thread. His results were published in 1882.

Mitosis

Eukaryotic cells have a nucleus. The nucleus must first divide before the rest of the cell can. Mitosis is the division of the nucleus. The subsequent division of the rest of the cell is called *cytokinesis*. First, the cell makes a copy of its **DNA**. Next, the cell goes through the following stages:

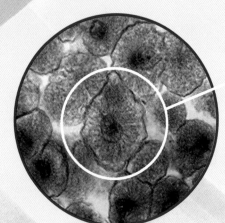

Prophase – DNA shortens and thickens to form chromosomes. The nuclear membrane disappears. The centrioles move to opposite ends of the cell.

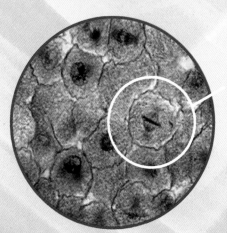

Metaphase – Long fibers extend from the centrioles and attach themselves to the chromosomes. The chromosomes line up in the center of the cell.

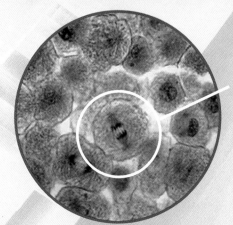

Anaphase – The fibers shorten and pull the chromosomes apart. The chromosomes begin to move toward opposite ends of the cell.

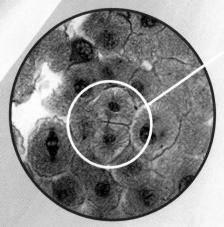

Telophase and **Cytokinesis** – The chromosomes reach the opposite ends of the cell. The nuclear membrane reappears around each new nucleus. The long fibers disappear. The cell splits apart and becomes two identical cells.

Mysterious Mitochondria

Mitochondria are fascinating organelles. They have their own separate DNA and ribosomes and they work independently of the nucleus. They also divide independently of the cell. Some scientists believe that millions of years ago, mitochondria were single prokaryotic cells living all on their own. Then, they were engulfed by larger eukaryotic cells, but not digested. Eventually, this resulted in the formation of a type of cooperative relationship. The eukaryotic cell provides the nutrients and the prokaryotic cell (now called mitochondria) converts these nutrients, providing the eukaryotic cell with its energy. Mitochondria are like cells trapped within cells.

CHAPTER FOUR

Impact of the Cell Theory

Shaping Science

The Cell Theory would have a profound and lasting impact on our world. It was a new way of looking at life. It unified the scientific world—a world that had been pulled in different directions by many conflicting ideas. The Cell Theory would provide a foundation for the understanding of disease, of evolution, and of the laws of heredity.

Quick fact

The ashes of a cremated person average about 9 pounds (4 kilograms). A big part of what gives the human body weight is the water trapped in our cells.

Hugo von Mohl

Hugo von Mohl was a German botanist born in 1805. The cell's nucleus had already been discovered and named by Robert Brown. But it was Mohl who suggested in 1844 that the nucleus was surrounded by something he called **protoplasm**. The term *protoplasm* comes from the Greek words meaning "first thing formed." Protoplasm is the slimy, fluid-like material inside the cell. Microscopes were not yet powerful enough to see all the tiny organelles in the protoplasm. They were, however, powerful enough for Mohl to observe how protoplasm behaved when a cell divided.

Historical Footnote

The plague, also known as The Black Death, was one of the most deadly diseases in human history. Between 1348 and 1350, it wiped out somewhere between 30 and 60 percent of Europe's population.

Development of Cellular Pathology

Pathology is the study of disease. Pathologists are scientists who look for the causes of disease. They also study the processes, the development, and the consequences of disease. By understanding the cell, scientists began to understand diseases in plants and animals a whole lot better. New medicines were developed. Doctors and scientists were better able to understand changes that happened in sick plants and animals.

They could also more easily and more accurately diagnose patients.

Remember Rudolph Virchow? He is known as the "father of pathology." Virchow believed disease came from individual cells. He believed there was a connection between strange activity inside cells and abnormal changes in the body.

↓These rice leaves have a fungal infection.

Hippocrates and the Four Humors

Long before Virchow, in ancient times, people of many different cultures believed you got sick because you were possessed by evil spirits or because you displeased the gods. Along came a Greek physician by the name of Hippocrates. Hippocrates was born in 460 B.C. He is considered the greatest physician of his time. Hippocrates believed disease had a physical explanation, not a superstitious one.

The Four Humors were special body fluids: blood, phlegm, yellow bile, and black bile. Hippocrates believed that a person's health, as well as their personality, was affected by these fluids. According to Hippocrates, disease came from an imbalance of these fluids. Rest, good diet, fresh air, and cleanliness were part of the healing process. This theory would be popular for centuries. Today, of course, our understanding of disease is much different. However, rest, good diet, fresh air, and cleanliness are still considered important to a person's health.

phlegm
(phlegmatic)

yellow bile
(choleric)

blood
(sanguine)

black bile
(melancholic)

↑ The four faces drawn here are intended to represent the Four Humors: blood, phlegm, yellow bile, and black bile.

Several hundreds of years later, in the mid-1800s, after Virchow had published his famous paper, "Cellular Pathology," scientists had begun to look at disease differently. According to Virchow, certain factors could affect cells and make them diseased. According to the Cell Theory, all cells came from already existing cells. This meant that diseased cells grew from already diseased cells.

Historical Footnote

Ships with crew members suffering from infectious disease hung a yellow flag as a warning. The ships were not allowed to dock for about 30 to 40 days.

Bacteria and Disease

Ferdinand Julius Cohn was a German botanist. Inspired by the discovery of Hugo von Mohl's protoplasm, Cohn was the first to define and classify bacteria. He is known as the founder of **bacteriology**. He was also the first to state that the protoplasm in plant cells and animal cells is pretty much the same. In 1872, he identified six separate classes of bacteria: Bacterium, Bacillus, Spirillum, Spirochaete, Micrococcus, and Vibrio.

Quick fact

Your tears and mucus actually break down the cell wall of many bacteria, destroying them.

Bacteria: Not Always the Bad Guy!

Bacteria are unicellular prokaryotic organisms. Most bacteria in our bodies are harmless—even helpful. You have more bacterial cells in and on your body than actual human cells! Bacteria help you digest your food, provide necessary nutrients, protect your skin, and contribute in many other ways to your health. Certain types of bacteria, however, can make you sick. Strep throat, scarlet fever, and pneumonia are diseases caused by bacteria.

Advances in Medicine

Cholera is a deadly infection that causes diarrhea, vomiting, and stomach cramps. Beginning in 1818, cholera killed hundreds of thousands of people. In 1854, John Snow, a scientist, linked cholera to drinking water. Snow suggested the disease was caused by **microbes** in the water. Many disputed his ideas. Thirty years later, a scientist named Robert Koch would support this hypothesis with strong evidence. Koch identified the actual bacteria that caused the disease.

↑Cholera outbreaks are often caused by contaminated water.

↑This bacterium, Vibrio cholerae, causes cholera.

"If my efforts have led to greater success than usual, this is due, I believe, to the fact that during my wanderings in the field of medicine, I have strayed onto paths where the gold was still lying by the wayside. It takes a little luck to be able to distinguish gold from dross, but that is all."

—Robert Koch, Journal of Outdoor Life (1908), 5, 164–9.

Anthrax

Anthrax is another deadly disease. Casimir-Joseph Davaine, a French doctor, was inspired by the work of Louis Pasteur. He was the first to notice tiny rod-shaped organisms in the blood of those suffering from anthrax. He conducted an experiment in 1863. He showed that sheep that did not have these organisms in their blood did not get anthrax. He also showed that if a cow was injected with even one millionth of a drop of blood containing these organisms, the cow got anthrax. Still, many were not convinced.

In 1875, Robert Koch would identify the bacteria responsible for anthrax. This was key evidence that there was a direct link between certain bacteria and certain diseases. His discovery was groundbreaking during a time when people were still arguing over the Cell Theory and spontaneous generation. It would also lead to the first **vaccines**.

Vaccines

Vaccines are tiny amounts of weakened or dead bacteria that are injected into people and animals. If the person or animal comes into contact with the same bacteria again, the person's or animal's body will know how to fight it. This is how you become **immune** to a disease. Louis Pasteur would create the first vaccines for **rabies** and anthrax.

Ancient Remedy

In China, many believe in the balance of two forces—*Yin*, the negative force, and *Yang*, the positive. If there is an imbalance of these within a body, a person becomes ill. To treat the imbalance, tiny needles are stuck into the body at certain points to increase the flow of Yin and Yang. This is called *acupuncture*. It is an ancient remedy still used today.

Human Cells

A human body is made up of several hundred different cell types. It would take a much larger book to talk about each distinct human cell type. But let's take a peek at some of the main cells in our bodies and the role the Cell Theory played in their discovery and understanding.

Blood Cells

Red blood cells have the very important job of delivering oxygen throughout your body. Their cytoplasm contains a lot of hemoglobin. Hemoglobin is an iron-rich molecule that makes your blood red.

↓ Red blood cells have a distinctive dimpled shape.

In 1695, Antonie van Leeuwenhoek was the first to describe red blood cells. But because the idea of the cell was still so new, no one, including Leeuwenhoek, seemed to think they were very important.

Decades would pass until an English surgeon, William Hewson, would think otherwise. In 1770, Hewson stated that because there were so many red blood cells in a body, they must play a very important role. For this reason, Hewson is known as the father of hematology—the study of blood.

Your blood contains more than just red blood cells. In 1842, a few years after Schwann's Cell Theory made cell study popular, a French physician, Alfred Donné, discovered another element to blood—**platelets**.

The following year, in 1843, Gabriel Andral, a French professor, and William Addison, an English doctor, were studying blood through a microscope. They simultaneously described white blood cells. White blood cells are what help you fight disease. If a germ or bacteria enters your body, your white blood cells go to work attacking these intruders. Sometimes, they give off powerful antibodies that overpower and destroy the bacteria. Other times, they surround the bacteria and actually devour it!

→ White blood cells, like these, help your body fight off disease.

Bone Cells

Bones protect your inner organs. They support you and give you shape. They allow you to move. Bone cells can grow and mend themselves. Many bones are hollow. Their hollowness makes them strong and light. In the center of these bones, something called **bone marrow** is hard at work. Bone marrow produces new blood cells.

Andrew Taylor Still was a physician born in Virginia, in 1828. After working as a surgeon during the American Civil War and after watching three of his children die of **spinal meningitis**, he began to study the human body. Still wanted to find new ways to treat disease. During this time, the **Germ Theory** was being developed—the idea that bacteria causes disease. Still rejected this idea. He opposed using vaccines. He became skilled at treating musculoskeletal problems. His advances formed the basis of osteopathy—the treatment of bones, uscles, and joints.

Quick fact

Humans shed about 600,000 skin cells every hour. The cells that form your stomach's walls are constantly replaced, too. You get a new stomach lining every few days!

Muscle Cells

There are three types of muscle cells: skeletal, smooth, and cardiac. Skeletal muscles are attached to your bones and help you move. Smooth muscles are found inside the walls of certain organs like your stomach. And cardiac muscle is found only in your heart. Your heart pumps blood through your body.

Skin Cells

Skin cells protect your internal organs from the cold, the heat, the rain, and the wind. Skin cells are flat. They are piled tightly against each other to form your tough exterior. To keep your skin in top form, skin cells flake off about once a month.

→This is a skin cell.

↑These are skeletal muscle cells.

←Skin is a barrier that protects your body.
Skin cells are replaced regularly.

The Transmission Electron Microscope

From ancient Greek times until 1897, the **atom** was thought to be the smallest unit of living and non-living matter. J.J. Thomson, a physicist, would prove everyone wrong. He discovered that atoms contained even smaller parts called **electrons**. In 1932, Max Knoll and Ernst Ruska developed a way to shoot these electrons through an object. This created a detailed image. And so the electron transmission microscope was invented. Today, the top electron transmission microscopes can magnify samples 50 million times their actual size!

Nerve Cells

Of all the human cells, the nerve cell is perhaps the most interesting. A nerve cell is also called a neuron. Neurons can process and transmit information using chemicals and electricity. Neurons branch out and connect to each other forming networks. They are what make up your nervous system. Your brain is made up of neurons.

During most of the nineteenth century, scientists debated about the nervous system. One group, the Reticularlists, led by Joseph von Gerlach, thought it consisted of a large network of tissue. Another group, the Neuronists, thought it was made up of individual cells. Although Schwann proposed the Cell Theory in 1938, most didn't think it applied to the nervous system. Microscopes weren't powerful enough to reveal the cellular organization of the nervous system so it would remain a highly debated topic for decades.

dendrites

↓Nerve cells are long, with branched ends. Their structure matches their function; nerve cells send and receive information, passing it from cell to cell.

nucleus

axon

axon terminal

Johannes Evangelista Purkinje

Johannes Evangelista Purkinje was born in Bohemia—now the Czech Republic—in 1787. He was an **anatomist** and one of the first to use the compound microscope. In 1832, he used a compound microscope to analyze nervous tissue. Purkinje is most famous for discovering cerebellar cells (now called Purkinje cells). He presented his research, which included detailed drawings, to the Congress of Physicians and Scientists in 1837. Because these cells are among the largest in the brain, they were the first neurons to be discovered.

Despite Purkinje's findings and many others, it was only at the end of the nineteenth century, as more powerful microscopes were developed, that scientists finally concluded that the brain consisted of individual cells. This vastly improved our understanding of the brain and led to advancements in neurology, the study of the brain.

Quick fact

Johannes Evangelista Purkinje was the first person to recognize that each person's fingerprints were unique and could be used for identification.

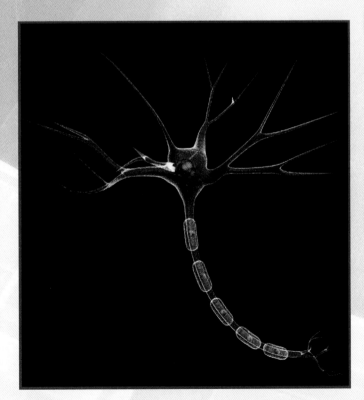

"Illusions of the senses tell us the truth about perception."

—Johannes Evangelista Purkinje

←Nerve impulses transmit information from neuron to neuron.

Fat Cells

Whether for health reasons or appearance, many people today are concerned about fat. But fat cells are important to the function of our bodies. Fat cells are like tiny sacs. They have less cytoplasm so that they have room to carry a tiny amount of fat. If you gain weight, you don't gain fat cells. Your existing fat cells simply get larger.

Energy in Cells

Your cells need energy to repair damaged cells, to grow, and to reproduce. Cells like a variety of food, including glucose (sugar), lipids (fats), and proteins. Molecules of broken-down food pass through the plasma membrane into the cell. After a cell consumes nutrients it changes these into energy. The energy produced is called **ATP**. ATP is to a cell what gas is to a car.

Cell Movement

As Antonie van Leeuwenhoek discovered, cells are not only alive, some of them move. Movement is important to many cells, but it is especially necessary for unicellular organisms. Without movement, they would have no access to food and oxygen.

Quick fact
Your brain is made up of about 100 billion nerve cells!

Quick fact
Every day your body makes about 300 billion new cells. Every month your outer skin cells have been completely replaced.

There are three types of cell movement. Some cells move using something that looks like a long, skinny tail. This tail is called a **flagellum**. These cells wiggle their flagella back and forth. The movement propels them forward. Other cells have cilia. Cilia look like fine hairs covering the outside of the cell. The cilia, like the flagella, wiggle. This motion can move the cell in all directions. Other eukaryotic cells appear to be crawling. They push all the jelly-like cytoplasm toward one spot. This makes a structure called a **pseudopod**, or "false foot." The foot anchors itself and then pulls the rest of the cell along with it.

↑ *This amoeba has a pseudopod extended.*

↑ *These cells look like they have tails—but their "tails" are actually flagella. Flagella help the cells move.*

CHAPTER SIX

The Importance of Chromosomes

Chromosomes are enclosed within the nucleus of a eukaryotic cell. In prokaryotic cells, they may be restricted to a region known as the nucleoid. Chromosomes carry a cell's genetic material, or DNA. DNA influences many characteristics of organisms, including appearance, behavior, and cellular chemistry. We didn't always know this.

Did You Know?

Typical human cells have 46 chromosomes. Potatoes have 48. Butterflies have 380.

Abnormalities in the chromosomes of a human cell can cause genetic disorders, such as Down Syndrome.

The Chromosomal Theory of Inheritance

Gregor Mendel was an Augustinian monk. Prior to his experiments, people believed that an offspring's traits were an in-between blend of both of its parents. For example, if a long-haired cat mated with a short-haired cat, the offspring would have medium-length hair. Mendel had other ideas. He believed what he called "factors" were responsible for the appearance of specific **traits**. In 1865, he conducted several experiments using pea plants. Mendel crossed yellow, smooth pea plants with wrinkly, green pea plants. Each time the offspring pea plants were yellow and smooth. In the second generation, however, some green and wrinkly peas resurfaced. Mendel showed that certain traits were **dominant** while others were **recessive**. However, Mendel's work remained unnoticed for some time.

In 1868, Charles Darwin published a hypothesis he called *pangenesis*. He believed units of hereditary information were collected inside the male and passed onto the offspring. In the 1870s, Darwin's hypothesis of pangenesis would be disproved by Francis Galton.

Then, in 1900, Dutch botanist Hugo de Vries published his research supporting what Mendel proposed 30 years earlier. De Vries shortened Darwin's word to *pangene* to describe what Mendel had called "factors." In 1909, Wilhelm Johansson would shorten the term again to **gene**.

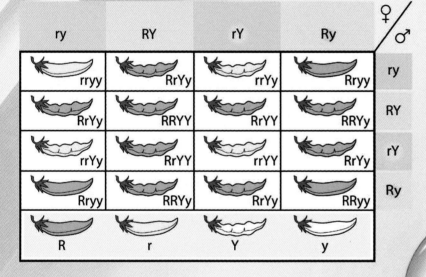

←*Mendel crossed two pea plants that had smooth green peas. He found that some of their offspring had smooth green peas, but others had wrinkled green peas, smooth yellow peas, or wrinkled yellow peas.*

Quick fact

All humans on the face of Earth are about 99 percent genetically identical!

"My scientific studies have afforded me great gratification; and I am convinced that it will not be long before the whole world acknowledges the results of my work."

—Gregor Mendel, 1883

Gametes and Sexual Reproduction

Human cells have two sets of 23 chromosomes—a total of 46 in each cell. But in certain cells, a process called *meiosis* takes place. This process produces cells that have only 23 chromosomes each—half the amount of other cells. These cells with half the amount of genetic material are known as **gametes**. In males, gametes are called *sperm*. In females, they are called *eggs*. When a sperm cell comes together with an egg cell, the new cell that is formed has all 46 chromosomes. By 1902, scientists knew the movements during meiosis. It begins with the cell making a copy of its DNA.

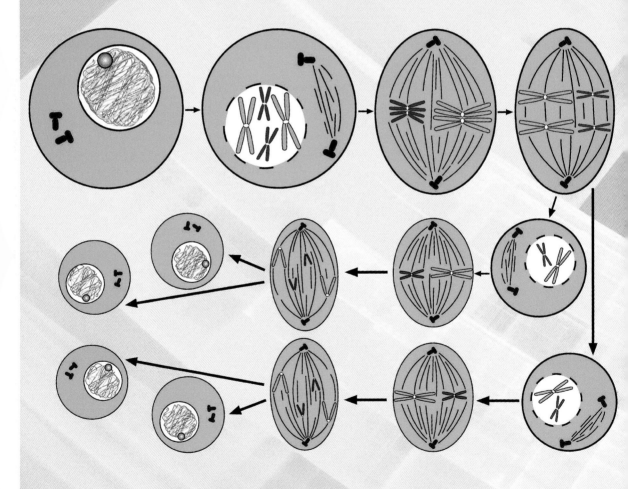

↑*Meiosis divides a cell's nucleus into four unique nuclei.*

Meiosis I

Prophase I – DNA shortens and thickens to form chromosomes. The nuclear membrane disappears. Centrioles move to opposite ends of the cell.

Metaphase I – Long fibers extend from the centrioles and attach themselves to the chromosomes. Pairs of chromosomes line up in the center of the cell.

Anaphase I – The fibers shorten and pull one of the matching pairs of chromosomes toward opposite ends of the cell.

Telophase I and Cytokinesis – The movement is complete. The nuclear membrane reappears around each new nucleus. The long fibers disappear. The cell splits into two cells, each of which contains 23 chromosomes. Notice at this point that the chromosomes are still duplicated. They do not duplicate again.

Meiosis II

Prophase II – The nuclear membranes in both cells disappear again. The centrioles move to opposite ends of each of the cells.

Metaphase II – Long fibers extend from the centrioles and attach themselves to the chromosomes. The chromosomes line up in the center of the cell.

Anaphase II – The fibers shorten and pull the duplicated halves of the chromosomes apart. The chromosomes begin to move toward opposite ends of the cell.

Telophase II and Cytokinesis – The chromosomes reach the opposite ends of the cell. The nuclear membrane reappears around each new nucleus. The long fibers disappear. The cell splits apart. There are now four daughter cells, each with only 23 chromosomes.

Genes and DNA

Chromosomes carry the cell's DNA. DNA is short for *deoxyribonucleic acid*. DNA is in the shape of a spiral ladder or staircase. It is about 1,000 times the length of the actual cell, so it folds into itself to fit inside the nucleus. If it were an actual staircase, it would be about 250 million steps. Sections of DNA are called genes. There are many genes on a single chromosome.

↓DNA is in the shape of a double helix. It is wound up and packaged into chromosomes, which are contained within the nucleus of a eukaryotic cell.

Differentiation

Humans have about 50 trillion cells. There are several hundred different cell types. But each cell in a person's body contains the exact same DNA. So what makes a skin cell a skin cell and a bone cell a bone cell? The answer is something called differentiation. Imagine your DNA is like a string of lights—each light represents one gene. Now imagine if on one string, only the first light is switched on and all others are off. Now imagine another strand where the first light and the last light are on and all others off. How about if only the first three lights were on? Or if every second light was lit? With 30 thousand genes, the possibilities seem endless. Switching certain genes on and others off is what turns one cell into a bone cell and another cell into a nerve cell.

Stem Cells

Stem cells are cells that have not had any genes switched on or off yet. They can become any type of cell in the human body. European scientists realized in the 1900s that all types of blood cells came from one particular "stem cell." But in 1963, after Canadian researchers Ernest McCulloch and James Till transplanted mouse bone-marrow cells and described their self-renewing activity, scientists realized the incredible potential of these cells.

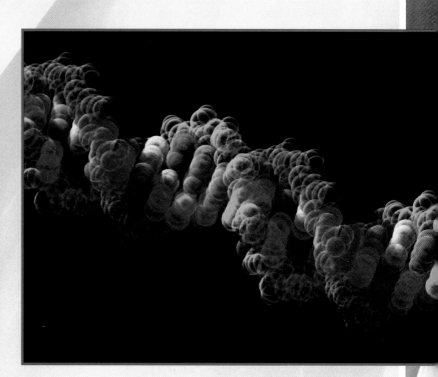

Discovering the Structure of DNA

Scientists knew about DNA for some time, but no one knew what it actually looked like. Then, in 1953, using information from Rosalind Franklin and other scientists, James Watson and Francis Crick made an incredible discovery. They figured out the structure of DNA. DNA is the shape of a twisted ladder. The rungs of the ladder are made up of combinations of four chemicals. These are called bases. Each rung of the ladder is made up of two of the four chemicals.

CHAPTER SEVEN

The Cell Theory Today

The main principles of the Cell Theory proposed long ago by Schwann, Schleiden, and Virchow still hold true today. But thanks to advancements in science and technology, there have been some refinements to the theory and more tenets have been added.

Changes in the Cell Theory

Two German botanists, Ludolph Christian Treviranus and Johann Jacob Paul Moldenhawer, were the first to propose the idea that cells could be divided into individual units. This led Henri Dutrochet, a French physician and botanist, to reformulate one of Schwann and Schleiden's original tenets. Instead of proposing that the cell is the smallest unit of life, Dutrochet stated that the cell was the fundamental unit of organization.

Beginning with Mendel and his pea plants and leading to the discovery of DNA and genes, another new tenet of the Cell Theory would be born. We now know that the cell contains hereditary information, which is passed from one cell to another when the cell divides.

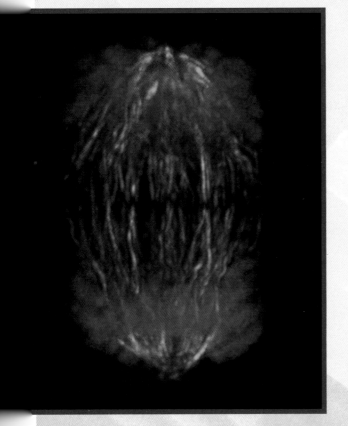

←Modern microscopy allows us to visualize, on a cellular level, the processes that account for the hereditary patterns that Mendel observed.

The Modern Cell Theory Has Six Principles:

- All known living things are made up of cells.

- The cell is the structural and functional unit of all living things.

- All cells come from pre-existing cells by cell division or through fertilization.

- Cells contain hereditary information, which is passed from cell to cell during cell division.

- All cells are basically the same in chemical composition.

- All of the energy flow of life occurs within cells.

Research into the cell continues and many new and exciting discoveries occur regularly. All new research springs from or is supported by the Cell Theory. It remains a foundation of modern **biology**.

Quick fact

Scientists have identified the entire DNA sequence of over 180 organisms, including humans.

The Human Genome Project

Genome is the word used to describe the entire collection of DNA that makes up a specific organism. In 1990, scientists embarked upon a great adventure called the Human Genome Project. They wanted to figure out the chemical code that made up every single rung of DNA in each human chromosome.

By doing so, they hoped they could make some significant changes and cure serious genetic diseases. The project was completed in 2003.

→ *The first printout of the human genome to be presented as a series of books.*

Contributions of Women

In early days, women were not considered equal to men. They were not allowed to attend universities. You may have noticed that all the early discoveries mentioned in this book were by men—there is a complete absence of women. This, however, has changed. Today, there are many women in the scientific community doing extremely important research, and who are credited with important discoveries. Here are just a few of them:

Elaine Fuchs is a biologist. She is the Rebecca C. Lancefield Professor of Mammalian Cell Biology and Development at Rockefeller University. She was the first woman in the biochemistry department at the University of Chicago in 1980. She is a strong supporter of women in science. Her work on skin disease has led to the modernization of dermatology. She also discovered skin stem cells.

Joan Wright Goodman was not only a pioneer in the field of stem cell research, she was a huge advocate of women in science. A brilliant woman who first attended law school before embarking on a scientific career, she was the first to discover that stem cells from bone marrow circulated in the blood of mammals. Her work remains central to stem cell research today.

Christiane Nüsslein-Volhard is a German geneticist. Along with Eric F. Weischaus and Edward B. Lewis, she was awarded the Nobel Prize in Physiology or Medicine in 1995. She conducted extensive research on the mechanisms of early embryonic development. Her work expanded on the work of Lewis, who used fruit flies as his subject. Her work is relevant to all multicellular organisms.

Rita Levi-Montalcini's father tried hard to discourage her from her interest in science. But after a friend died of cancer, she decided to attend medical school just the same. She would eventually work alongside Stanley Cohen. The two would discover something called Nerve-Growth Factor (NGF) and Epidermal Growth Factor (EGF). The duo won the Nobel Prize for Medicine in 1986.

"Senior women who are recognized by their peers as being successful have a responsibility to help educate those scientists who haven't quite accepted this important message. . . Leading by good example is still the best way to diffuse the now more subtle and less vocal, but nevertheless lingering, discrimination and dogmatism against women scientists within our scientific community."

—Elaine Fuchs, 2004

Quick fact

In the 1930s, food in Italy was scarce. After conducting experiments on chicken embryos, Rita Levi-Montalcini would cook and eat the remaining yolks.

Cloning

Cloning is the technique of removing the nucleus from an egg cell and replacing it with the nucleus of an adult cell. The embryo is then implanted into a surrogate mother. The mother gives birth to an organism identical to the adult nucleus-donor. In 1952, the first animal was cloned. It was a tadpole, but it didn't survive long. In 1996, a sheep was cloned. Scientists named her Dolly. She survived and went on to have offspring.

Creating Artificial Cells

In 2007, Craig Venter, one of the researchers involved in the Human Genome Project, stitched together chemicals and actually built a synthetic chromosome. It was 381 genes long and contained 580,000 base pairs. Venter claims it was "the creation of the first new artificial life form on Earth."

↑These wheat seeds were genetically engineered to withstand a fungal disease.

Genetic Engineering

Genetic engineering is the science of altering the DNA of organisms. It can mean removing a piece of DNA from a living thing. It can also mean taking DNA from one living thing and placing it into another. By doing this, scientists make changes in living things. For example, they have removed genes from bacteria that produce poison, and inserted them into corn plants. The resulting corn plants have their own built-in pesticide. They have added a worm gene to pigs so that the pigs produce omega-3 fatty acids found in fish. They have also placed spider genes into goats. The goats produce spider silk protein in their milk. It is called BioSteel™ and is ten times stronger than actual steel. The curious list goes on.

The Future of Cells

With everything we already know about the cell, it is hard to believe just how much there is left to discover. Researchers are hard at work uncovering new and exciting things each day. Our limits extend only as far as our imaginations.

Quick fact

In 1982, scientists developed a new, risk-free way to make insulin. By placing human DNA inside bacteria cells, scientists "tricked" the bacteria into making human insulin. This has helped countless people all over the world who suffer from diabetes.

Cancer Cells

Typical cells reproduce exactly and stop reproducing at the right time. They stick together at the right place and they self-destruct if they are damaged. Cancerous cells don't stop reproducing. They don't stick together and they don't obey the messages sent to them by other cells. Worst of all, they don't self-destruct.

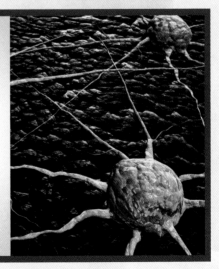

Timeline

1595 Zacharias and Hans Janssen develop the first compound microscope.

1628 William Harvey describes blood circulation.

1655 Robert Hooke describes "cellulae" in cork.

1661 Marcello Malpighi describes pulmonary capillaries.

1674 Antonie van Leeuwenhoek sees "animalcules" in fluid samples.

1695 Antonie van Leeuwenhoek describes red blood cells.

1770 William Hewson decides red blood cells are actually important.

1831 Robert Brown sees a spot in cells of orchids and names it "nucleus."

1832 Barthélemy Dumortier observes cell division in plants.

1837 Johannes Evangelista Purkinje identifies cerebellar cells.

1838 Theodor Schwann, expanding on Schleiden, proposes the Cell Theory.

1842 Alfred Donné discovers platelets.

1843 Gabriel Andral and William Addison independently discover white blood cells.

1844 Hugo von Mohl discovers protoplasm.

1858 Rudolf Virchow states that cells develop only from existing cells.

1863 Casimir-Joseph Davaine identifies rod-shaped organisms in the blood of sheep with anthrax.

1865 Gregor Mendel conducts experiments on pea plants.

1868 Miescher isolates DNA from pus cells of old bandages.

1872 Ferdinand Julius Cohn identifies six classes of bacteria.

1875 Robert Koch identifies bacteria causing anthrax.

1882 Flemming publishes what happens to chromosomes during mitosis.

1900 Hugo de Vries publishes his work supporting Mendel.

1932 Max Knoll and Ernst Ruska make the first prototype of the transmission electron microscope.

1953 Using Franklin's images, Crick and Watson propose the structure of DNA.

1963 Ernest McCulloch and James Till transplant mouse bone marrow cells.

1980 Elaine Fuchs is the first woman in the biochemistry department at the University of Chicago.

1982 Insulin is made using human DNA inserted into bacteria.

1995 Christiane Nüsslein-Volhard wins the Nobel Prize for Medicine.

1996 Dolly, the first cloned sheep, is born.

2003 The human genome is sequenced.

2007 Craig Venter creates a synthetic chromosome.

2010 New DNA test developed for early detection of colon cancer.

Glossary

anatomist An expert in the structure of living things

anthrax A deadly disease caused by bacteria and spread by spores

archaea Single-celled prokaryotic organisms without a nucleus but different from bacteria

arteries Blood vessels that carry blood away from the heart

atom A basic unit of matter

ATP Stands for "adenosine triphosphate" and is a high energy molecule that fuels the cell

bacteria Organisms consisting of a single prokaryotic cell

bacteriology The scientific study of bacteria

bias To hold to a certain perspective while dismissing any possible alternatives

biology The study of life and living things

bone marrow A soft, fatty tissue that fills most bones

botanist A person who studies plants

cell wall The exterior surface of prokaryotic cells and eukaryotic plant cells

chloroplasts Organelles found in plant cells that are responsible for capturing light energy and, through the process of photosynthesis, turning this into energy for the plant

chromosome Thread-like structure that contains a cell's DNA; in eukaryotic cells, chromosomes are found in the nucleus

compound microscope A microscope with more than one lens

cytoplasm The jelly-like substance inside a cell

cytoskeletons The structure that acts like the cell's skeleton

DNA Molecules that contain the instructions for making new cells

dominant The type of trait that will appear in the offspring if one of the parents contributes it

electron A particle within an atom that carries a negative electric charge

endoplasmic reticulum A network of membranes running through the cell

epithelial Refers to the cells that line or cover organ surfaces, such as the surface of the skin, or the lining of the digestive tract

eukaryotic A cell having a true nucleus

flagellum A tail-like structure that helps certain prokaryotic and eukaryotic cells move

gamete A reproductive cell that has half the typical number of chromosomes

gene The basic unit of heredity made up of a section of DNA

genetic material Anything from a small piece of DNA to the entire genome of an organism

Germ Theory The theory that infectious diseases are caused by microorganisms, such as bacteria

Golgi apparatus Part of a cell involved in secretion and protein modification

hypothesis An explanation for an observable phenomenon or scientific problem

immune Being protected from getting certain diseases because of a natural resistance to the disease, or a resistance after already having had the disease or because of a vaccination

lipids Fats

membrane An outer layer of the cell, the nucleus or other organelles that acts as a barrier

microbes A very tiny life form, such as bacteria

microscopist A person skilled in the use of the microscope

mitosis The division of a cell's nucleus

molecules The smallest units of a substance

multicellular Made up of more than one cell

nucleoid Large space inside prokaryotic cells that contains genetic material

nucleus Membrane-bound part of the eukaryotic cell known as the control center

organelles A specialized unit inside a cell that performs a specific function

organisms Living things

organs A collection of tissues that join together to perform a specific function; for example, the heart or the lungs

photosynthesis A process in green plants that converts energy from sunlight into substances like sugar that serve as energy for the plant

physicist A scientist who studies physics

physiological Related to the science that studies the normal functions of living things or their parts

plasma membrane Exterior surface of eukaryotic cells

plasmid A circle of DNA found in bacteria

platelets Clear cells found within blood that do not have a nucleus containing DNA

Glossary continued

postulated Suggested as a basis for discussion

prokaryotic A cell that does not have a true nucleus

protoplasm The term first used to describe the substance inside a cell (later called "cytoplasm")

protozoa Single-celled eukaryotic organisms

pseudopod A temporary projection of cytoplasm that helps certain cells move

pulmonary capillaries A network of blood vessels in the lungs where oxygen and carbon dioxide are exchanged; they connect the pulmonary arteries to the pulmonary veins

rabies A viral disease that causes inflammation of the brain

recessive A word that describes a gene that is hidden by a dominant gene

ribosomes Parts of the cell that build proteins

semi-permeable Something that blocks certain molecules but allows others to pass freely

spinal meningitis A sometimes fatal disease in which the membranes enclosing the spinal cord become inflamed

spontaneous generation The idea that living things can originate from non-living matter

theory A concept or idea that is supported by all known scientific evidence

Theory of Evolution The idea that populations change over generations through a process called natural selection

traits Distinguishing features

unicellular Made up of only one cell

vaccines A substance injected into a living thing to protect it from certain diseases

vacuole A compartment in a cell that stores nutrients, waste products, or substances to be secreted

veins Blood vessels that carry blood back to the heart

For More Information

Books

Allman, Toney. **Great Medical Discoveries: Stem Cells**. Lucent Books, 2006.

Dowdy, Penny. **Animal Cells (Let's Relate to Genetics)**. Crabtree Publishing, 2009.

Dowdy, Penny. **Plant Cells (Let's Relate to Genetics)**. Crabtree Publishing, 2009.

Hyde, Natalie. **DNA (Let's Relate to Genetics)**. Crabtree Publishing, 2009.

Hyde, Natalie. **Traits and Attributes (Let's Relate to Genetics)**. Crabtree Publishing, 2009.

Sherman, Josepha. **How Do We Know the Nature of the Cell (Great Scientific Questions and the Scientists Who Answered Them)**. Rosen Publishing Group Inc., 2005.

Websites

www.cellsalive.com   Everything you ever wanted to know about cells

www.kidsbiology.com/human_biology/index.php
   See photos of cells from all parts of the human body.

www.biology4kids.com   Learn about cells and take a quiz to test your knowledge.

http://science.howstuffworks.com
   Information about many science topics—plus a science dictionary

http://dsc.discovery.com/tv/human-body/explorer/explorer.html
   Videos, games, and a lot more—all about the wonders of the human body

http://yucky.discovery.com/flash/body/
   The science behind body functions, both gross and cool

Index